Holiday Histories

# Memorial Day

Mir Tamim Ansary

**Heinemann Library**
**Chicago, Illinois**

© 1999, 2006 Heinemann Library
a division of Reed Elsevier Inc.
Chicago, Illinois

Customer Service  888-454-2279
Visit our website at www.heinemannraintree.com

Designed by Kimberly Miracle and Q2A Creative
Printed in China by South China Printing Company

10
10 9 8 7 6 5 4 3

New edition ISBNs:        1-4034-8890-8 (hardcover)     978-1-4034-8890-9 (hardcover)
                          1-4034-8903-3 (paperback)     978-1-4034-8903-6 (paperback)

**The Library of Congress has cataloged the first edition as follows:**
Ansary, Mir Tamim.
     Memorial Day / Mir Tamim Ansary.
        p. cm. -- (Holiday histories)
     Includes bibliographical references and index.
     Summary: Introduces Memorial Day, explaining the historical events behind it, how it became a holiday, and how it is observed.
     ISBN 1-57572-874-5 (lib. bdg.)
     1. Memorial Day – Juvenile literature. [1. Memorial Day. 2. United States – History – Civil War, 1861-1865. 3. Holidays.]  I. Title. II. Series: Ansary, Mir Tamim. Holiday histories.

E642 .A57 1998
394.262 – dc21
                                    9814377

**Acknowledgments**
The author and publishers are grateful to the following for permission to reproduce photographs: Center Daily Times p. 28-29; Corbis p. 5 (Paul Barton); The Granger Collection pp. 9 (right), 10, 11, 12, 13, 14, 16 (all), 20, 21, 22; John Andress p. 23; Magnum Photo p. 7 (Eugene Richards); Mississippi Department of Archives and History p. 24 (left); Photo Edit p. 24 (Gary Conner); Photo Researchers, Inc. p. 9 (left); Stock Boston p. 6 (John Loletti); SuperStock pp. 8, 10, 15, 19, 26; Theater Pix p. 27 (Michael Brosilow).

Cover photograph reproduced with permission of Jim Corwin/Alamy.

# Contents

Some words are shown in bold, **like this**. You can
find out what they mean by looking in the glossary.

# A Day for Remembering

Memorial Day is the last Monday in May. Flowers are blooming. The school year will be over soon. It is a fine day for outdoor fun.

But there is another side to Memorial Day. This holiday is about remembering. On this day, we remember people who died in wars.

# Memorial Day Customs

Many Americans put flags and flowers on graves of people who died for our country. This family's loved one died in the Vietnam War. He died in 1970.

This family's loved one died in World War Two. He died in 1944. His family still decorates his grave on Memorial Day. It is an old **custom**.

# The Roots of a Holiday

Memorial Day goes back to the Civil War. That was the biggest war ever fought on U.S. soil. The Civil War ended in 1865.

A Union, or Northern, soldier

A Confederate, or Southern, soldier

In the Civil War, Americans fought Americans. Our country had split in two. The North fought the South. The fight was about **slavery**.

# Freedom and Slavery

The United States was **founded** as a land of freedom. But there was a problem from the start. Some people in the United States were **slaves**.

**Slavery** was allowed in the Southern states. The South had big farms. On those farms, slaves did most of the work.

# A Nation Torn

**Slavery** was against the law in the North. Most people in the North felt slavery was wrong. Many wanted to **ban** it in all states.

Every time a new state joined the country, the question was asked: Should slavery be allowed here? Fights broke out over this question.

# Civil War

In 1860 the Southern states tried to leave the United States. They said they were a new country. They bombed a U.S. fort.

Abraham Lincoln was president then. He said
our country was a **union**. No state had a right
to split away. He sent armies to fight the **rebels**.

# The Battle of Gettysburg

The South had a great general named Robert E. Lee. Lee drove the **union** armies back. Then he **invaded** the North.

A big battle took place near Gettysburg, Pennsylvania. It lasted three days. More than 43 thousand men died or were hurt. Lee's army was driven south again.

# Lincoln's Greatest Speech

President Lincoln went to Gettysburg. He gave a **speech** to **honor** the dead. He explained what the men had died for.

Lincoln said the United States stood for a great idea: Every person is born equal and free. If the country split, he said, this idea would die.

# The Tide Turns

After the Battle of Gettysburg, the North also found a great general. His name was Ulysses S. Grant. He began wearing down the **rebels**.

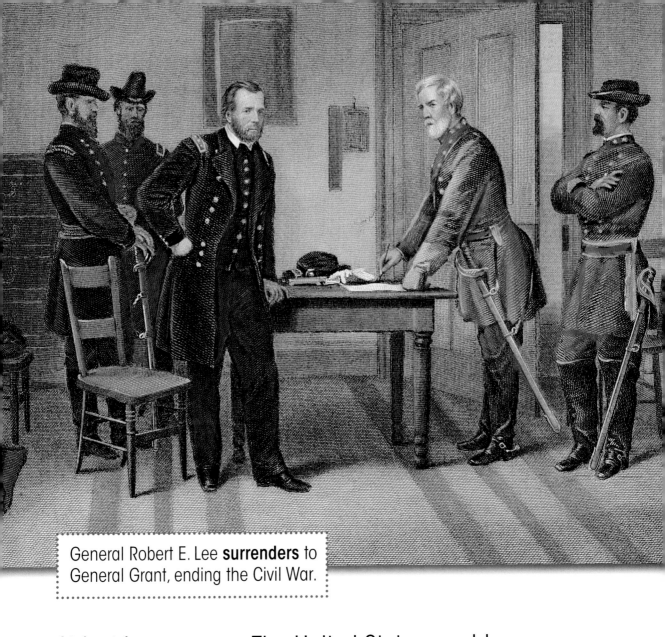

General Robert E. Lee **surrenders** to General Grant, ending the Civil War.

At last Lee gave up. The United States would stay together as one country. And no one in this country would be a **slave**.

# Healing the Wounds

But how could people in the North and South be friends again? The war had left so many people hurt. It had left so much hate.

One day a group of women went to a cemetery in Columbus, Mississippi. Soldiers from both the North and South were buried there. The women did something wonderful.

# Memorial Day Begins

The women put flowers on the soldiers' graves. They did not ask which side they fought for. They **honored** all the soldiers.

This picture shows the women who helped start Memorial Day.

People in other towns copied this idea. That is how Memorial Day began. In 1971 it was made into a national holiday.

# Memorial Day in Our Time

Memorial Day **honors** all who have died in our country's wars. There is a big **ceremony** at the national cemetery in Arlington, Virginia.

Small ceremonies take place across the country.
People put flowers and tiny flags on graves.
Some **mourn** in private.

# Sadness and Joy

But Memorial Day is not just a sad time. Many towns have festivals on this day. Here is a big festival in Boalsburg, Pennsylvania.

Festivals like these mix joy with sadness. They
remind us of a good thing on this day in May.
Spring and summer always come again.

# Important Dates

## Memorial Day

| | |
|---|---|
| **1776** | The United States is **founded** |
| **1860** | South Carolina leaves the **Union** |
| **1861** | The Civil War begins |
| **1863** | Battle of Gettysburg takes place |
| **1864** | Ulysses S. Grant takes charge of the Union armies |
| **1865** | The Civil War ends |
| **1866** | Women decorate graves in Columbus, Mississippi |
| **1945** | World War Two ends |
| **1971** | Memorial Day is declared a national holiday |
| **1975** | The Vietnam War ends |

# Glossary

**ban**      make something against the law

**ceremony**      special activity to honor someone or something

**custom**      something people always do on special days or for certain events

**founded**      set up something new, such as a country

**honor**      show respect for someone

**invaded**      entered a land or country by force to take over

**mourn**      feel or show sadness about a loss

**rebels**      those who fight against their government

**slaves**      people who were forced to work for other people and were owned, bought, and sold like property

**slavery**      use people as slaves

**speech**      talk given to a crowd of people

**surrenders**      gives up

**union**      group of many parts that works together; Northern states during the Civil War

# Find Out More

Burke, Rick. *Abraham Lincoln.* Chicago: Heinemann Library, 2003.
Frost, Helen. *Memorial Day.* Mankato, Minn.: Capstone, 2000.
Schaefer, Ted and Lola Schaefer. *Arlington National Cemetery.*
     Chicago: Heinemann Library, 2006.

# Index